SNOW BORNE SOUVENIRS

Verses from winter's heart.

Shruti Kaul

BookLeaf Publishing

Presentation by *BookLeaf Publishing*

Web: www.bookleafpub.com

E-mail: info@bookleafpub.com

ISBN: 9789363307827

First edition 2024

Dedication & Acknowledgement

The creation of "Snow Borne Souvenirs" has been a deeply personal journey, through what feels like several lifetimes. I extend my heartfelt thanks and dedicate this book to my parents and late grandparents who instilled perseverance and resilience in me, that has helped me through upheavals, difficult times, grief and fleeting momentous joys of life. And lastly, in contrast to most acknowledgements, I would like to thank myself for my strength, my patience, my learning and growth and my courage during all these times that helped me shape these verses into this collection and share it with you all.

Contents...

Preface...

I was born in Srinagar, Kashmir, on one of the heaviest snowfall days that year. Not a single soul would have fathomed back then, that this white cold will engulf my heart and life in the years to come. My poignant memories—or souvenirs as I like to call them, are borne by my snow-clad world, with fragments of hope and warmth my heart still holds on to. And reminiscing and longing for the same warmth of the kangari my mom, grandmom and aunts used to prepare for me and my cousins, to keep us warm during the winter months, all throughout my childhood and teenage years.

"Snow Borne Souvenirs" is a mosaic of the memories that have left an indelible mark on my heart and soul. Each souvenir evokes deep emotions that capture the elusive connection between the snow's cold quiet majesty and the rich tapestry of experiences it inspires. This collection reflects my journey through the snowbound landscapes of memory. Each verse seems to whisper the tales of yesterday, making the past feel both distant and intimately close.

This collection is not just a chronicle of my personal history, but a reflection on the universal human experiences of memory and nostalgia. I hope that by sharing these stories, readers will find echoes of their own lives, and perhaps, rediscover their own treasured souvenirs from the past, yet holding on to the love and hope for the future.

Words...

Words change so often,
Memories shake so often!

It's not about the lies,
It's about the truth so often.

It's not about the meanings,
It's about the meaningless so often.

It's not about the destiny,
It's about the dreams so often.

It's not about what's said,
It's about what's unsaid so often.

It's not about remembering,
It's about forgetting so often.

Words change so often,
Memories shake so often!

A Ray of Hope!

Nothing to express,
Nothing to say,
Is it just me,
Or it's the haze?

Can't see the light,
Can't see the day,
Now I know,
The essence of a ray!

A lot to come,
A lot that went,
It ain't that easy,
The way it felt!

Listening to people,
Listening to god,
Wish it could be me,
Who's saying it all!

It's been long,
It's too late,
Since I last tried to paint;

The colours have whisked off,
The paper is pale,
Yet it's the hope,
That makes life sail!

Waiting for the Day!

I am swaying with the wind, ready to be carried
away,
I am loving the night, but waiting for the day!

I ceased from the wanderings, and laid still,
I breathed long and thought of a song,
I could hear the tears and the silent fears,
I wished for wings and I wished for miracles,
I was lost in slumber like a fly in amber,
I chose to wake up and shun the dreams,
I am not afraid of the waves or the dark caves,
I am like a clod but watched over by god,
I can be an ocean and I can be a pond,
I can be a breeze and I can be a storm,
I know the screams and the hidden forlorn,
I walk on a path over the sand dunes,
I know it can slide or end near a moon,
I choose to walk past the stark landscape,
I am waiting for the exuberant light and the
epiphany,
I am loving the night, but waiting for the day!

Daydreaming...

We start by dreaming,
Of the fairytales and the neverlands,
Of all that's white and lights with a wand;
Deeper the skies and joyous the bands!

We start by dreaming,
Of the heavenly love and the magical doves,
Of the rivers blue and the flowers that bloom;
Magic's the trick and the mirrors in the room!

We end waking up,
To the edge of the world;
Of the thoughts that are hazy and life's a hearse,
Of the nights that are silent and days are a curse,
Patience's the word and the time's the traverse!
We start by dreaming!

Humans!

We are so fickle and fragile,
Broken by hearts and lifted with smiles!

We are divine with riches,
Or else it twitches;

We are shiny trophies,
And can be seen as showpieces;

We burn to end up strong,
And yet break down when things go wrong;

We are so beautiful outside,
And yet have voids inside;

We are so fickle and fragile,
Broken by hearts and lifted with smiles!

The Lost Boat.

A tardy boat lost in the sea,
The shore's afar, where it wishes to be,

The waves and the tides push it deep,
Oh! The winds and the sky won't set it free,

The sails are torn and look forlorn,
No one to steer and no direction's clear,

It moves on and beyond,
Past the islands and the reefs,

It will find the shore or merge with thee,
A tardy boat lost in the sea!

The Endless Search.

When we have wandered too far,

When we have dived too deep,

When we have gazed too long,

When we have searched too hard,

When we have lost so much,

When we have gathered so less,

We find it all, when the soul introspects!

The Water Colour Life.

Looks picture-perfect with mesmerizing
insights,
The merging colours look like gleaming lights;

The story unfolds like a magical sight,
Each drawing is worth a million smiles;

But for a splash of water, lest it be ruined,
The paper soaks all the colours within;

All is in the paper, yet nothing prevails,
The remnants pose a stark landscape;

It seems like a rainbow, just dispersed in rain,
Our water-coloured lives smeared with pain!

Is It Just Me?

A thousand words,
And none I say,

A thousand scenes,
And none I see,

A thousand memories,
And none I share,

A thousand scars,
And none I bare,

A thousand noises,
And silence is all I hear!

An Optical Illusion!

All these years I was buried deep in the ground,
The soil had covered all my wounds,

My soul was reposing from all the strain,
I wished tomorrow would have no restraints,

As I watched the clouds and far beyond,
I wished for the day, I would rise from the
ground,

The way you swayed me, I felt so light,
As if the morning breeze dusts off the night,

Your gleamy light filled up my eyes,
My soul never felt so alive,

Your smile emanates like the sunshine,
I can gaze at you till the end of time,

You mean the world to my life,
The reason I rose from all the strife,

We may not have traversed too far and along,
But only to you, I belong,

You shall be in my heart remember,
Cause darling I love you, forever and ever!

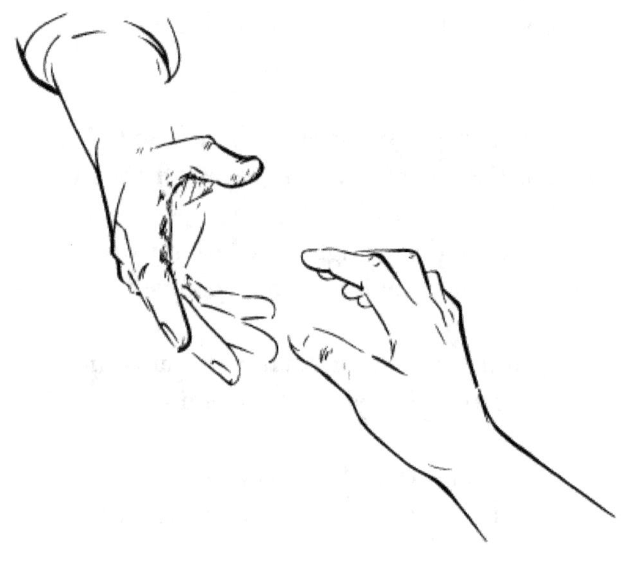

The Yearning!

With all the agony I can bear,
The twinges in my heart that pierce,

The noises with every breath I hear,
My soul churned and stirred,

Sing me a requiem if you care,
The dead may rise from the holy sphere,

The soil might swill all our tears,
Our minds free from all the fears,

Our eyes attain the transpired dreams,
Our hearts rescued with incandescent beams,

For the souls know no deceits,
For love can conquer all extremes!

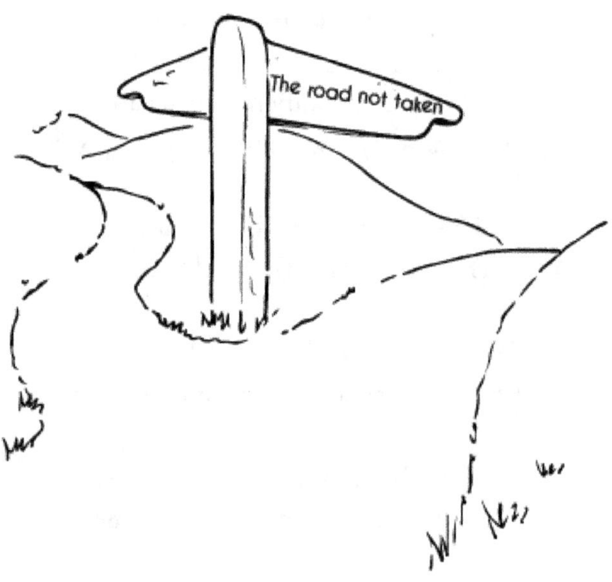

The road not taken

The Path We Choose...

The mystery of words lies in our minds,
The imagination seeks no advice,
The heart can guide through the uncertain
skies,

The wolves howl for it's the feeding time,
The one we feed is the one we tread,

The past grief dismantles the present,
The door we seek is the one we shut,

The words take over at the mind's bchest,
The soul knows the truth and can transcend,
The paradise is raised with love, efforts and
intent!

The Gold Seeker!

For he who seeks just the outside,
Mostly holds a preposterous mind,

For he values just the glitter and the glint,
For the kind soul is unknown and unkempt,

It may dissipate at the smallest behest,
Or stay strong during a conquest,

For he who doesn't value the inner shrine,
Finds solace in all the lies,

The soul turns ugly but the outer shines,
For the mirror can't reflect what's hidden
inside!

The Colours Of Our Life.

So far you've lived all the colours of life,
The bright, the pale and the light,

Though it seems like a lifetime,
It's only just been a while,

Though it might seem nowhere,
It would eventually lead you there,

Though it's whimsical and mysterious,
It has the magic hidden somewhere,

Though it might not be a rainbow or the shades
of vivid,
Only you know what colours you liked and
what colours you lived!

All Conditions Applied!

Oh! If the imperfections would cease to exist,
the particles of our existence would dilute in the
mist;

The cluster of clouds our world has got,
would it be any different if they dispersed
around;

The shining light that the sun brings along,
burns the other side of the ground;

The life we measure by different amounts,
is getting shorter by leaps and bounds;

All the myths that swallow the heart,
feed on the people who follow their path;

The ocean never fears any storms,
and the queer water can take any form;

The night intensifies the dark,
yet few souls shine like stars!

The Burial!

A storm wrecked room,
Memories in the loom,
Paintings of the stars,
Drowned in tar,
All the books on the shelves,
Turned into char,
A garden full of bloom,
On a sunny afternoon,
Wilds growing tall,
Covering all the roots,
Rainy days ahead,
Looking for a shed,
Like the stones in the streams,
Lay me down near the trees,
Let me soak in the shades,
Before I head back to the bees,
Let the remains be laid,
In the growth they aid,
All the shrugs rise back,
To lay their claims,
What belongs to the earth,
Has been restored!

A Winter Wonderland.

The dancing stars make your heart flutter,
The lights afar seem a little better,

The shooting stars make you wish harder,
Is it a knight in the shining armour or a
cataclysmic dishonour?

Will it protect you forever, or will it bury you
deeper?
Will it pass by, by the speed of light, or grasp
you and hold you tight?

Will you reach the skies of the universe?
Or will you break apart in the cosmic wars?

Is it a deadly weapon, meant to destroy your
little heaven?
Or is it the peace you were searching for?

Falling all over like the crystal drops,
Covering you in little shiny orbs,

Oh! To feel all that and yet wander,
Some hearts are meant to tatter,

Hope it heals in this starry realm,
Hope it feels like a euphoric triumph,

Hope it stays till the end of time,
Burning bright through the darkest of the
nights!

The Cycle...

In the spring rain, when the flowers bloom,
In these drops, we can see the moon,

There goes the chill, breaking my spine,
The cold air drying my vines,

Some wishing me buried in the ground,
Or maybe the sun would burn my shroud,

I kept walking, looking at the cloudy skies,
Thinking what are we made of and what
becomes when one dies,

The water is pure, pouring from the clouds,
It takes you back and sifts you out,

There's a journey for every dead,
They can look back or trudge ahead,

The dark forest swallows the best,
But some find the leeway steps,

The slippery path leads to a shed,
Some get a grip, some slide and skid,

As you pushed her aside,
Yet couldn't be safe in your pride,

As you wither in pain,
Washing away in the rains,

Life's a lesson of what one does and repays,
Last summer she bled, this spring you ache!

The Journey!

All the shores I walked, the seas were afar,
I laid on the sand, as the swim was a war,

The sweet sounds of the ocean dilated with
whims,
The gales so high, they tore my shins,

I found a lighthouse through the squall,
As calming as the sky, as shining as the opal,

I wondered if it's real,
Or am hallucinating from the ordeal,

The freezing water and a bout of flu,
A concoction of sensations that I never knew,

It's the warmth of the summer and the delight
of the dews,
Like a breeze lingering around, bringing scents
from the ground,

A blooming spring, in the midst of a drought,
Serenading me with its views, not just red, but a
bevy of hues,

A bewitching tale of twenty years,
A candid frame of unbeknownst flares,

Tears apart, through mountains and hearts,
Floating buoys on the waves of shards,

Treading back in the time capsule,
Heading to the shore, we were meant to choose!

Silence!

For in our silence, we hear, the loudest noises of
our wounds,

For in our silence, we lay to rest, our parts that
have been bruised,

Our deepest desires we had to lose,

For in our silence we grieve, the souls we lost,

Our heart that never heals and the ache we feel,

For in silence, we pray, for the ones who
betrayed,

For the homes we thought we would make,

For the times of despair, for our body that's
frayed,

And our soul on spears,

For in silence, we wish them, happiness and
bliss,

For the words fall short and weak, yet in our
silence, we speak!

The Ocean Like Life.

At the surface, there's a calmness that descends,
There's silence in the wind and peace within,

There's a brightness when we gaze and a
sheen-like haze,
But when we look deep inside, the mirror
reflects our plight,

We were naive and oblivious to the fate,
We thought life was just harnessing the waves,

But the currents, the moon and the creatures
alike,
Create a storm that devours the light,

Many lives are lost and many reefs crumble,
They take years to form and seconds to rubble,

And yet the vastness absorbs all the sounds,
The stillness holds every rebound,

The noises merge with the shore,
No cries can ever be heard,

And the unrest can't be seen with the naked
eyes,
As the ocean puts up a mesmerizing disguise!

Glossary

Bare: Open to view-exposed.

Behest: An authoritative order-command, or an earnest request.

Bevy: A large group of similar things.

Bewitching: Enchanting or delightful.

Bout: A short period of illness.

Buoys: A floating object on the top of the sea, used as navigation marks.

Cataclysmic: A momentous and violent event marked by overwhelming upheaval and demolition.

broadly-an event that brings great changes.

Char: To convert to charcoal or carbon usually by heat-burning.

Churned: To have an unpleasant disturbed feeling. To move or cause to move about vigorously.

Clod: A lump of earth or clay.

Concoction: A mixture of various ingredients or elements.

Descends: To move down a slope. To move or fall downwards.

Devours: To destroy something completely.

Emanate: Give out or emit (a feeling, quality, or sensation).

Epiphany: An intuitive grasp of reality through something (such as an event) usually simple and striking.

Euphoric: To feel intense happiness and excitement.

Exuberant: Produced in extreme abundance.

Fickle: To change your opinion or your feelings frequently or suddenly and without a good reason.

Flares: A sudden burst of intense emotion.

Flutter: If your heart flutters, it beats faster than usual, often from excitement.

Forlorn: Pitifully sad and abandoned or lonely.

Frayed: Damaged, weakened, or worn down by strain or irritation.

Gales: A very strong wind.

Gleaming: Shine brightly, especially with reflected light.

Glint: Small, bright flashes of light reflected from a surface.

Hallucinating: To experience an apparent sensory perception of something that is not actually present.

Harnessing: To control something, usually in order to use its power.

Hearse: A vehicle for conveying the dead to the grave.

Incandescent: Intensely bright, radiant, or clear.

Leeway: Room for free movement within limits.

Lingering: Lasting for a long time or slow to end.

Loom: A machine that is used for weaving thread into cloth.

Neverland: An imaginary place where everything is pleasant or perfect in a way that is impossible to achieve in real life.

Oblivious: Not aware of or conscious about what is happening around you.

Opal: An opal is a precious stone. Opals are colourless or white, but other colours are reflected in them.

Orbs: Something in the shape of a ball.

Preposterous: Contrary to reason or common sense; utterly absurd or ridiculous.

Queer: Strange; odd.

Rebound: To bounce back after hitting a hard surface. To recover from setbacks or frustration.

Remnants: A small piece or amount of something that is left from a larger original piece or amount, a surviving trace.

Reposing: Lie down in rest.

Requiem: A musical composition in honour of the dead.

Rubble: Broken bits and pieces of debris left after demolishing or destroying anything.

Serenading: To play a piece of music or sing for someone, especially for a woman while standing outside her house at night.

Shards: A piece of broken ceramic, metal, glass, or rock, typically having sharp edges.

Shin: The front part of the leg below the knee.

Shroud: A layer of something that covers or surrounds something.

Sifts: To go through especially to sort out what is useful or valuable. To cause to flow or pass through a sieve.

Smeared: A dirty mark made by spreading a liquid or a thick substance over a surface.

Squall: A sudden violent gust of wind or storm, especially one bringing rain, snow, or sleet.

Stark: Empty, simple, or obvious, especially without decoration or anything that is not necessary. Severe or bare in appearance or outline.

Strife: Trouble or discord of any kind.

Swaying: To move or cause to move slowly backwards and forwards or from side to side.

Swill: Wash or rinse out by pouring large amounts of water or other liquid over or into it.

Tar: A dark, thick flammable liquid distilled from wood or coal.

Tardy: Delaying or delayed beyond the right or expected time; late.

Tatter: Torn in many places; in shreds.

Transcend: To triumph over the negative or restrictive aspects of any limit.

Transpired: Something previously secret or unknown becomes known.

Traverse: To move or travel through an area.

Treading: Walk on or along.

Trudge: To walk slowly with a lot of effort, especially over a difficult surface.

Twinges: A sudden, sharp, brief feeling of pain or an emotion.

Twitches: A short, sudden jerking or convulsive movement to a part of the body.

Unbeknownst: Happening or existing without the knowledge of someone.

Unkempt: Crude, in a natural or raw state; not yet processed or refined.

Vines: A plant whose stem requires support and which climbs by tendrils or twining or creeps along the ground.

Vivid: (Of a colour) intensely deep or bright.

Whims: A sudden desire or change of mind, especially one that is unusual or unexplained.

Whimsical: Subject to sudden change; unpredictable. Unusual and strange in a way that might be funny or annoying.

Whisked off: To take or move (someone or something) somewhere suddenly and quickly.

Wither: To slowly disappear, lose importance, or become weaker.

Yearning: A feeling of intense longing for something or someone.